This book belongs to:

Published by iDisciple Publishing
2555 Northwinds Parkway, Alpharetta GA 30009

ISBN: 978-0-578-78470-0
Printed in China

Author: Katie Kenny Phillips
Illustrator: Mieke van der Merwe

JESUS Loves EVERYBODY

KATIE KENNY PHILLIPS
Illustrated by Mieke van der Merwe

God sent
Jesus to love
everybody.

When He was born,
He was a sweet little baby.

But not everyone loved Jesus—in fact, there were people who hated Him.

Even though there was hate in the world,
Jesus was sent to love everybody.
And so He did.

Jesus met a lot of different people.
And He loved them all.

Even stinky fishermen.

He loved big crowds of hungry people.
And bold children who shared their things.

Small groups of
scared people.

And people who wanted
to be brave for Him.

Jesus loved sick people who couldn't get better. People who couldn't see. Couldn't speak. Confused people who couldn't think straight and people no one would touch.

Angry people.

Happy people.

People who looked different from Him.
And people who looked the same.

Jesus loved people who couldn't walk and people who were courageous for their friends.

Jesus loved people who made bad choices.

And people who made good ones.

He loved everybody—
even the sorry ones.
And the suspicious ones.

Jesus loved those who were poor.
And those who were rich.
And everyone in between.

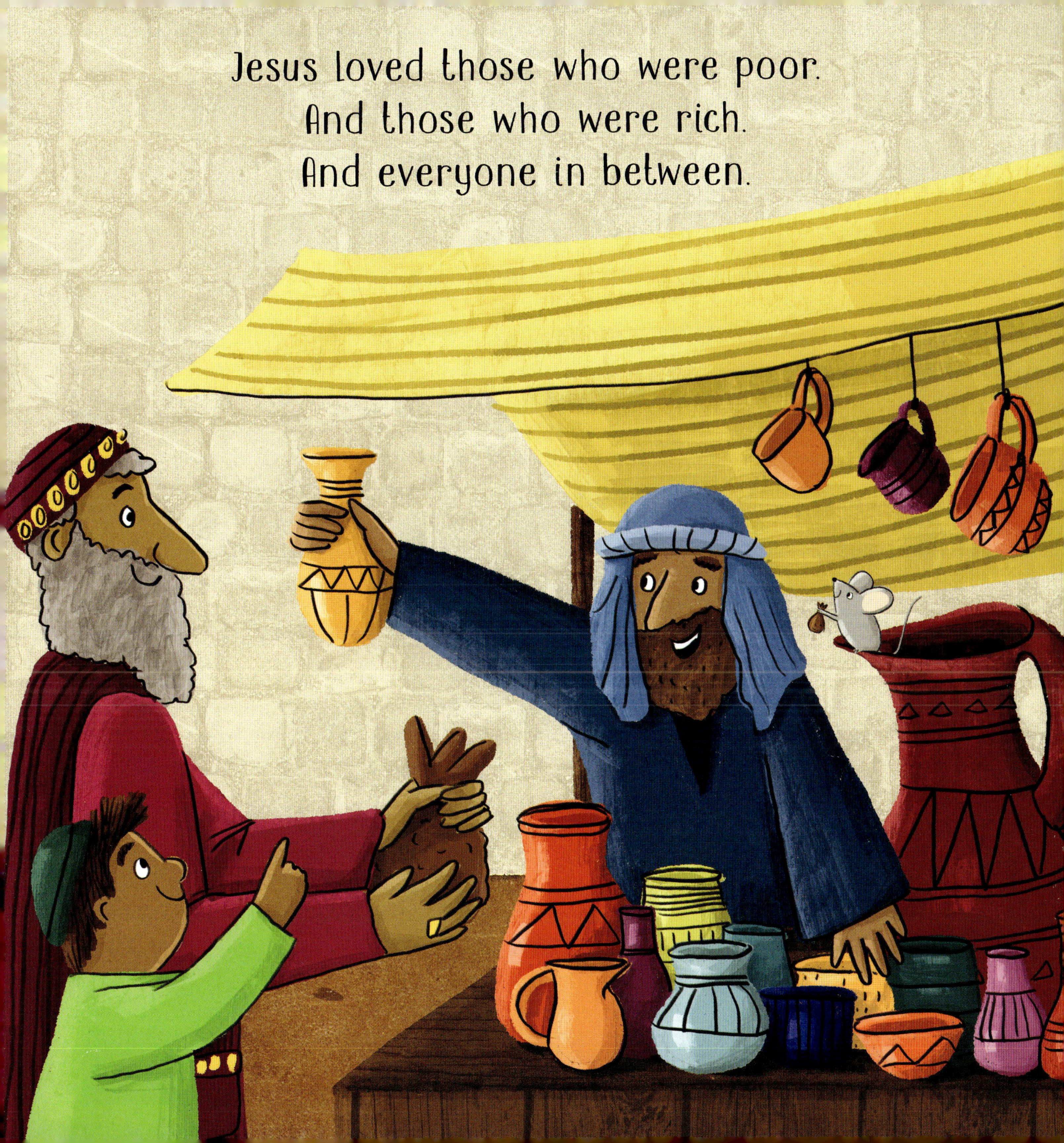

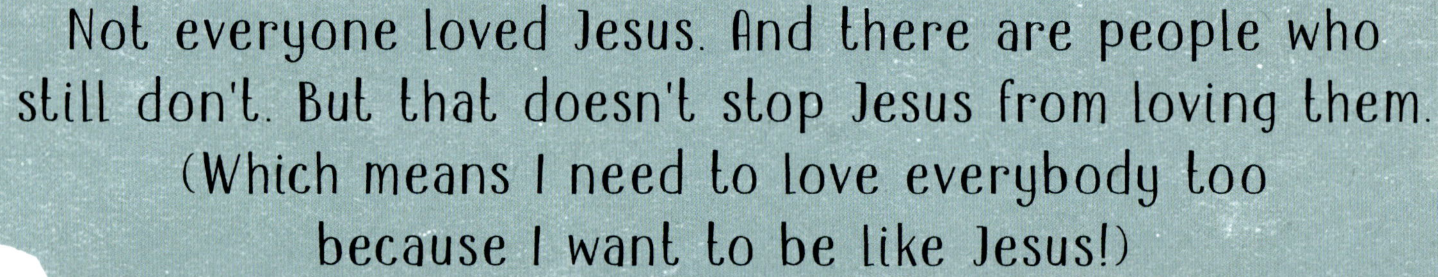

Not everyone loved Jesus. And there are people who still don't. But that doesn't stop Jesus from loving them. (Which means I need to love everybody too because I want to be like Jesus!)

Even if people don't look or sound like me. Even if they have a different skin color. Even if they are taller or shorter or silly or serious! I need to remember one important thing: Jesus loves everybody.

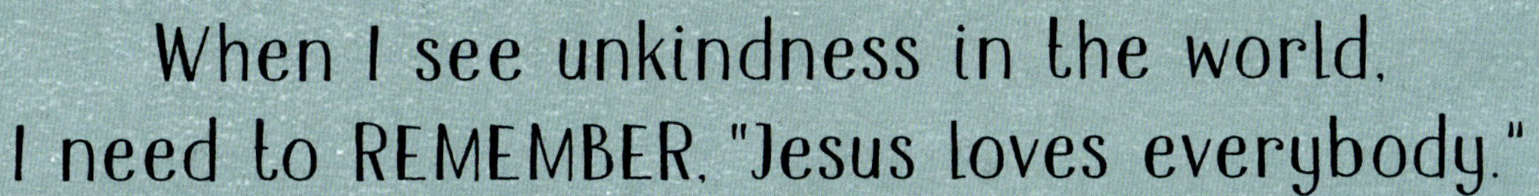

When I see unkindness in the world,
I need to REMEMBER, "Jesus loves everybody."

When I see ugliness and hate in the world,
I need to STAND UP and say, "Jesus loves everybody!"

When I see anyone who is different than me,
I need to remember ... Jesus.
Because Jesus loves everybody.

And so should I.

"My command is this:
Love each other as
I have loved you."

- Jesus

(John 15:12 NIV)

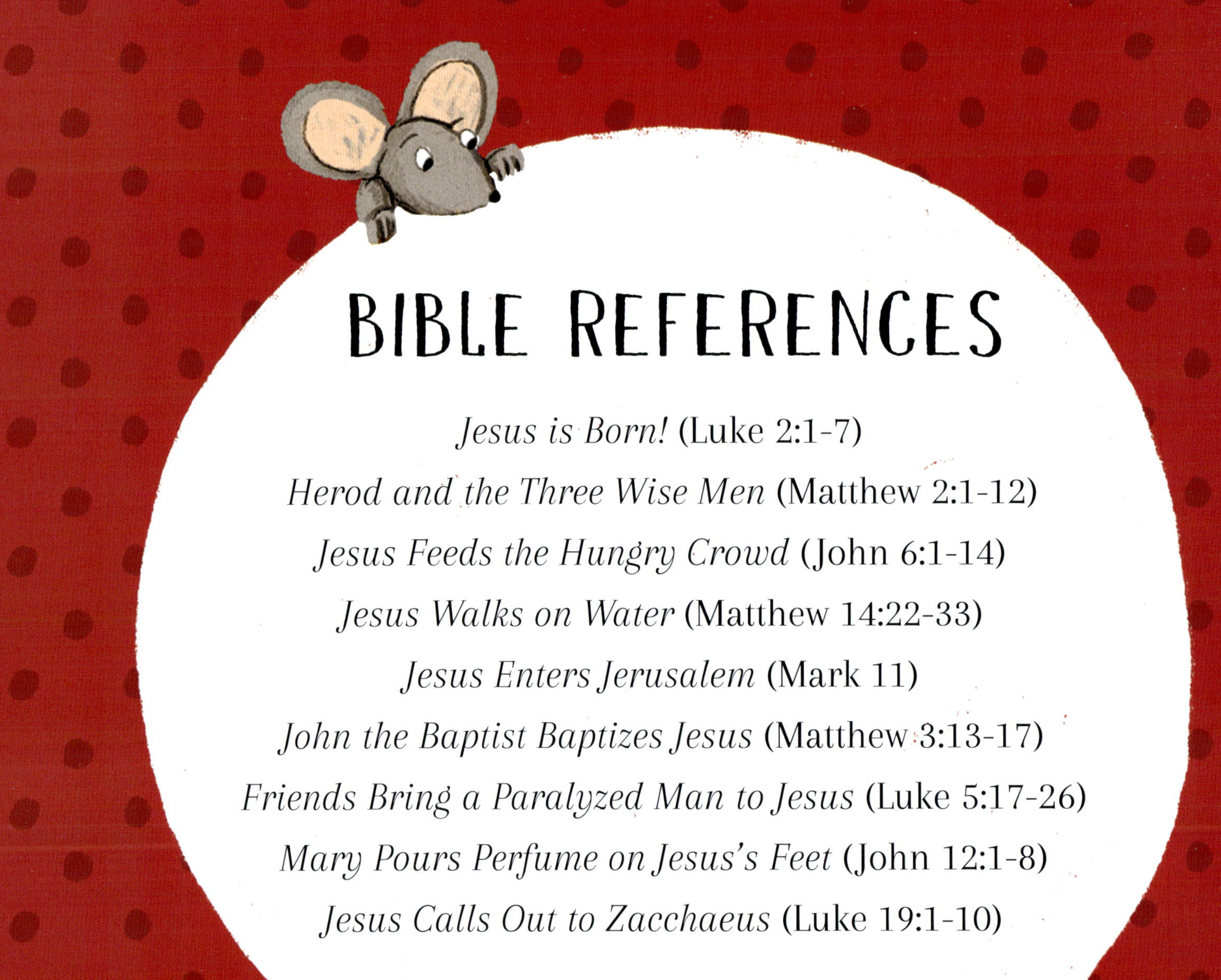

BIBLE REFERENCES

Jesus is Born! (Luke 2:1-7)

Herod and the Three Wise Men (Matthew 2:1-12)

Jesus Feeds the Hungry Crowd (John 6:1-14)

Jesus Walks on Water (Matthew 14:22-33)

Jesus Enters Jerusalem (Mark 11)

John the Baptist Baptizes Jesus (Matthew 3:13-17)

Friends Bring a Paralyzed Man to Jesus (Luke 5:17-26)

Mary Pours Perfume on Jesus's Feet (John 12:1-8)

Jesus Calls Out to Zacchaeus (Luke 19:1-10)